The Freeway to Happiness

by
Pat Davis

Authors Choice Press
Bloomington

The Freeway to Happiness

Copyright © 2008, 2011 by Pat Davis

Authors Choice Press
an imprint of iUniverse, Inc.

iUniverse books may be ordered through booksellers or by contacting:

iUniverse
1663 Liberty Drive
Bloomington, IN 47403
www.iuniverse.com
1-800-Authors (1-800-288-4677)

ISBN: 978-1-4620-0047-0 (sc)

Printed in the United States of America

iUniverse rev. date: 04/14/2011

DEDICATION

I would like to dedicate this book to my mother and father, who practiced positive thinking throughout their lives and passed this philosophy on to me. It is never too late to learn this, as you will carry this optimism and truth forever.

I am 76 years young and I further dedicate this book to all those whom I have met in my lifetime, as I have learned something wonderful from each one of you.

TABLE OF CONTENTS

PART ONE – FAMILY 11

Abiding Love on Your Anniversary 12
Merry Christmas, Mom 13
Rules of the Road 14
My Sister, Evelyn 15
My Brother, Johnny 16
Our Lenka 17
Bryan 18
My Friend Mike 19
Parents 20
Greg 21
Merry Christmas, Dad 22
The Doll 23
Determination Pays Off 24
Children Building 25
Our Little House 26
His Friend, Teddy 27
When a House Became a Home 28
"Taps" for a Fallen Hero 29
Spanish Village by the Sea 30

PART TWO – SEASONS 31

Our Friends, the Seagulls 32
The Torrential Rain 33
Vacation Time 34
My Valentine 35
My Little Snowman 36
Wondrous Cycle 37
Weather 38
The Ocean of Love 39

When the Sky Is Crying 40
Our Great Seasons 41
Nature's Birthday 42
Have You Ever Seen? 43
The Desert Rats 44
Your Special Gift 45

PART THREE – TECHNOLOGY 47

My Little Computer 48
My Remote 49
Television Sets 50
Hear Ye, Hear Ye! 51
Our New Car 52
Telephone Calls 53
Automation 54
That Little Cell 55
This Little Card 56

PART FOUR – BELIEFS 57

Your Belief 58
Some People Say 59
Being Wise Brings Happiness 60
Greatest Sound of All 61
Thankful 62
God's Wrath 63
Health, Wealth, and Happiness 64
The Whisper 65
My Star 66
Positive Attitude 67

PART FIVE – TRAVEL. 69

Troops in War 70
Clickety-Clack, Clickety-Clack 71
My Daily Walk 72
The Sheriff 73

PART SIX – DITTY/STORIES 75

Shopping Spree (a Ditty) 76
Time 77
The Concerned Bystander 78
Realization! 79
The Wise Woodsman 80

PART SEVEN – SPORTS. 81

The Newcomer 82
It's Only a Game 83
The Wise Hunter 84

PART EIGHT – PUZZLES 85

Jigsaw Puzzle of Life 86
Which One Are You? 87
Love Is? 88
Another New Adventure 89

PART NINE – LIGHTHOUSES 91

The Lighthouse of Life 92
My Love for Lighthouses 93

PART TEN – MISCELLANEOUS 95

The Policeman 96
Good Ole USA 97
Hair 98
The Captain and His Dog Toot 99
Appreciate What We Have 100
Your Mystery Book 101

PART ELEVEN – EPILOGUE 103
Epilogue 104

THE FREEWAY TO HAPPINESS

The Freeway to Happiness

The freeway to happiness costs not a dime,
You'll travel many roads and you'll have a great time.
You can't see or touch it, but your heart will sing,
The freeway to happiness is a wondrous thing.

The freeway to happiness is a miracle to behold,
Age is no barrier, as you can be young or old.
The highway may be rough, curvy, smooth, or straight,
You'll find that this long freeway is positively great.

You may travel so fast that it takes your breath away,
As you become older, a month seems like a day.
If you really believe that this freeway is true,
You'll find that happiness that was meant for you.

This long freeway is not hard to find,
Because by now you realize it comes from the mind.
You'll be a positive thinker all your life through,
The happiness you'll want will always be with you.

PART ONE

FAMILY

Abiding Love on Your Anniversary

You both fell in love many years ago,
Then you watched your children grow.
Your love deepened as time went by,
You know your love will never die.

And now you're older and you can see
How your love and life was meant to be.
It must have come from Heaven above,
That what's known as abiding love.

Merry Christmas, Mom

Outside the snow and cold wind blows
Gifts are wrapped with ribbons and bows.
Houses are decorated with love and grace
Beautiful scenery is all in place.
Children are excited by the colors and lights
They are trying to be good, not many fights.
All parents are hoping that this peace lasts
At least until Christmastime has passed.
But lo and behold, as most children do
They're right back at it and come to you.
You're cooking, cleaning, and shopping for gifts
Stop what you're doing to solve all tiffs.
The children start playing with the new toys
You see your husband become one of the boys.
The dinner is over and the kitchen is a mess
Who cleans it up? You only need one guess.
It's done with love, but please never fear
You get to do it again the very next year.

Rules of the Road

A boy and girl holding hands as they crossed the street,
The parents watching them, as it was such a treat.
Both children were laughing when they saw a big old car,
The driver put on his brakes and didn't go too far.

He gave a wave and smiled and motioned them to go ahead,
The parents followed and waved at the polite driver and said,
"Thank you for stopping and waiting for all of us to cross."
He said, "That's okay, I'm not in a hurry, so there's no loss."

At home, the children were asked what they had learned today,
"A nice man followed the rules, even if we did play."
The pleased parents asked, "What else did you learn?"
In unison they both said, "Traffic is everyone's concern."

My Sister Evelyn

I have an older sister as sweet as she can be,
She's truly a lady as anyone can see.
I wanted to be just like her, but no matter how I try,
To be like her is like trying to reach and touch the sky.

Her penmanship is beautiful and she is very bright,
Everything she touches seems to come out just right.
She can sew or plant flowers, even cook a mean steak,
She can do it all without even one mistake.

She raised her family and is loved by one and all,
Even though she's retired, she keeps busy and has a ball.
A very kind and witty lady that I love and admire so,
Even though she may be quiet, she is always on the go.

She works jigsaw and crossword puzzles in her spare time,
She lives with my older brother and they get along fine.
I wrote this little poem, as I wanted her to know,
Just how much I miss her and how I love her so.

My Brother Johnny

I have an older brother that I love very much,
He is very kind and thoughtful and has a soft touch.
He's smart and loving as only he can be,
The nicest man that anyone would ever see.

He was in the navy and fought in World War II,
Then became a teacher and taught public school.
He raised his family and now is retired,
He is truly someone that is highly admired.

I wish all could meet him and then you would see,
Just why he means so very much to me.
When I am with him, I am happy and have a ball,
I think of him often, so I have to give him a call.

He's witty and quite a fellow, as all who know him see,
He lives across the country quite a distance from me.
So I wrote this poem just to let him know,
How much I miss him and how I love him so.

Our Lenka

There's a hardworking lady that cleans our home,
It is to her we dedicate this poem.
She's beautiful and friendly and very kind,
She thinks of others all of the time.

She has to leave us, but she'll come back,
We will miss her and that's a known fact.
We wish her well in all that she may do,
If you're her friend, she will be true to you.

She will be happy, no matter come what may,
We will think of her often, at least once a day.
She has a keen sense of humor, that is true,
She's emotional, as that's her nature too.

Now it's time to say so long for now,
We know she'll come back to us somehow.
So our dear friend, please remember us do,
As every day, we will be thinking of you.

Pat Davis

Bryan

A little boy was born in November,
He's one person you'll always remember.
Now he's older, he is the best man ever,
When you meet him, you'll love him forever.

A great father, there is no doubt,
He works very hard as he travels about.
If you ever need him, just give him a call,
He'll be there for you, he will not let you fall.

When you are sad, he'll give you a lift,
For his sense of humor is his greatest gift.
Bryan will make you smile and cheer you up,
And joy and laughter will fill your cup.

My Friend Mike

I have a friend that is loyal and true,
She's wise and smart and thoughtful too.
Loves her children and grandchildren all,
She laughs a lot and has a ball.

We met about forty-four years ago,
And traveled together, going to and fro.
We lived our way to the golden years,
We are here today and still no tears.

We've slowed down just a little bit,
We know we are old, but we are still fit.
They tell us that we're in the golden years,
We smile, clink our glasses, and down a few beers.

But don't be sad 'cause that's a waste of time,
I am still having fun with that best friend of mine.
We're not ready to leave Earth and wave bye,
We decided she's not going and neither am I.

Parents

Who said "Mommy?" I do not know,
I turned around, but where did she go?
"Wait for your daddy and say it again,
Then you can say 'Daddy' to that big ole man."

"Daddy is here now, so show off your trick,"
The girl didn't say a word and I felt sick.
"Go ahead, say 'Daddy'," I urged her on,
But she crawled away and she was gone.

I went to be by her daddy's side,
"She doesn't like me!" aloud he cried.
"Don't feel bad and don't be blue,
Your little daughter really does love you."

The next morning, our daughter yelled,
"Daddy, Daddy!" and his heart swelled.
"That's my girl" he said with a grin,
From then on, mommies can't win.

Greg

A caring man is in my life, my dear friend is his mother,
He is the youngest of two and he loves his older brother.
If you need him, he will be there giving a helping hand
And when you are with him, then you will understand.

He has responsibility, but he doesn't seem to mind
But that's only his nature just to be so kind.
If you are sad, he'll cheer you, even make you smile
And when you are with him, you'll laugh in a little while.

He is smart and sensible; if you need advice, just ask,
His logical mind will think about it, then take on the task.
This great man is a special father and husband so true
And if you ever meet him, he'll be a good friend to you.

Pat Davis

Merry Christmas, Dad

You start to mumble 'cause you know
Putting together toys is no way to go.
Where are the batteries and all those tools?
Whoever made these things were surely fools.
Package says follow directions to the letter
I don't need those 'cause I can do it better.
But why is one wheel higher than the other?
A wheel fell off, better call my brother.
Mom just smiles and says she doesn't mind
Knows that is the blind leading the blind.
You work half the night, directions unread
Mom just shrugs and then goes to bed.
It's Christmas Eve and you gotta hurry
You and your brother are beginning to worry.
It's early morning, about five minutes to four
Mom sees you're both asleep on the floor.
Directions are laid out in a straight line
You did this with love and toys work fine.

The Doll

There was a beautiful doll sitting on a stand,
Dressed all in pink and her dress was grand.
A little child looked at this lovely thing,
And then this little girl began to sing.

She could not carry a tune, not at all,
But she wanted to sing to that little doll.
The store owner looked up and to her surprise,
The little girl had big tears in her eyes.

"What's wrong?" the owner asked, trying to be sunny.
"I would buy this doll, but I have no money."
Owner said, "Please don't cry, and please don't pout."
The little girl turned and ran right out.

She came in again and pointed and said,
"That is my sister and she is now dead."
The owner gave the doll to this little tyke,
As she noticed they looked exactly alike.

Determination Pays Off

A little girl playing in the sand,
Trying to put it gently into a pail.
She scoops it up with one hand.
Determined she will not fail.

Sometimes she misses the little pan,
But she just laughs and continues on.
She really tries the best she can,
But opens her hand and says, "All gone."

The little pail seems to never get full,
She tries again, but to no avail.
The other hand gives the container a pull,
It tips, and there is no sand in the pail.

On her tiny face there is a little smile,
She makes a tight fist full of sand.
She reaches over and after a while,
The bucket is full and all is grand.

Children Building

Two young children were building a sandcastle on the beach,
The waves were coming in, but it was out of reach.
They built many rooms and around them, the walls were high,
They found they couldn't get out, they gave a mournful sigh.

The little girl and her brother were trapped inside the wall,
They just laughed and laughed as it didn't matter at all.
On a nearby blanket, their parents watched all the fun,
To their surprise, the building of a door had just begun.

They worked so hard to make the sandy door just right,
The children even argued and got into a fight.
Their parents didn't interfere, as they wanted them to learn,
It's good to ask directions, it might solve that certain concern.

All of a sudden, the door came off and the children were saved,
They wanted to show their parents how good they had behaved.
They stuck out their chests, each with a smile on their face,
For they knew they solved the problem, so there is no disgrace.

Pat Davis

Our Little House

We live in a little house that stands proudly on a hill,
In the early morning, it becomes quiet and still.
We can see the rolling hills and the ocean blue,
The flowers bloom in force and the birds sing right on cue.

We love this little space, as it's warm and friendly too,
There are such lovely neighbors, I know this to be true.
It's where we hang our hat and we will never leave,
This is our heaven on Earth, that we do believe.

When you live in a place that you adore,
You really can't ask for anything more.
And when the sun sinks low in the sky,
Then you'll know you'll be content until you die.

I love this little house we call our place,
It's a memory we'll not ever erase.
So drive on up and come right on in,
An experience you can't lose, you will only win.

His Friend Teddy

There was a little teddy bear sitting on the chair.
He was soft and round, as he had lots of hair.
A little boy came scurrying up to see his little friend.
He took him off the chair and Teddy's life came to an end.

The little boy didn't mean to, but he dropped him on the floor
And Teddy fell all apart just as his dad came through the door.
The little boy started to cry as his friend was really sick.
He thought he should be punished, so he got his father's stick.

The father looked into teary eyes of his precious son.
He left the room and got a Teddy that was a much better one.
The little boy sniffled, and gave his dad a weak smile,
For he knew this one was well and would last a long while.

Pat Davis

When a House Became a Home

There is a beautiful house but not a soul is there
It's just an empty shell 'cause there's no one to care.
People came to see and find the beauty of this place
But no one took a chance to make it their home base.
A family came to look at it, but then they went away
This house wished that they would hurry back to stay.
Each residence needs a loving family, that you can't deny
And because it's so lonely, this house began to cry.
One day some people came to look at this property
The house began to smile when it saw this family.
There was a warm feeling in the whole house through
This family knew there was something they had to do.
They talked and thought it over and lo and behold
That beautiful house on the corner was finally sold!
Now it's their true home and all are happy as can be
For this house became a home and it suits them to a T.

"Taps" for a Fallen Hero

To all those who fight for us

The morning was quiet and air was very still
A captain lay beneath the earth on a distant hill.
Slowly, a young bugler started in to blow
"Taps" for this fallen hero as he was honored so.
One early morning, this battle had begun
Our soldiers were outnumbered by ten to one.
The enemy moved forward, a fierce battle did ensue
Our troops fought hard for our red, white, and blue.
The captain fired his rifle and some say that he had said
You'll not get my men and flag, for you will all be dead!
The enemy was defeated, all his men he did save
But this courageous captain was sent to an early grave.
Men stood at attention as "Taps" began to play
Brave soldiers were crying and they begin to pray.
So when we hear "Taps" played across our promised land
Think of those who died for us and you will understand
Why these men are loyal to this hero in every way
But "Taps" is played too often in our USA today.

Spanish Village by the Sea

To the people in my city

There is a growing city that lies beside the sea
It's our special little place called San Clemente.
The schools are terrific and the weather is best of all
It's where fish are plentiful and healthy trees grow tall.
Boats come from many places to enjoy the ocean blue
If you ever come to visit, you will love this place too.
Spanish Village by the Sea was its name, so they say
It was changed to San Clemente as it is known today.
There are many little shops along the street Del Mar
All the people are friendly in this greatest city by far.
We have a marvelous street fair that is special to behold
For miles around visitors come, as it's for young and old.
Different types of restaurants provide a tasty treat
There is a beautiful pier where the surfers go to meet.
The houses are built for families and senior citizens too
This is heaven on Earth and it's here for me and you.
The sunsets are so beautiful, they take your breath away
And the views of hills and ocean are always here to stay.
The birds love this paradise as they fly up above
When this land was put here, it must have been with love.

PART TWO

SEASONS

Our Friends, the Seagulls

For my friend Mike

If you're ever at the beach, you'll hear the seagulls' call
Dressed in white tuxedos, but they don't mind at all.
Our friends are not afraid of us as they land by our side,
Hoping we'll drop some food before the evening tide.
They perch by people fishing even from a pier,
And if we are not careful, the fish might disappear.
These seagulls are very friendly and care for us a lot,
They watch us in fascination, wondering why we like it hot.
They watch us roasting our body on blankets in the sun,
The children chasing seagulls and all are having fun.
They wonder if it's liquid food we spread on our skins,
Then they see some funny people wearing rubber fins.
They watch surfers on a board riding waves and then,
The riders fall into the water and go right back out again.
Theses humans are a strange lot as anyone can see,
Our friends, the seagulls are more tolerant than we.

The Torrential Rain

The rain is really falling down,
The umbrellas are up all round the town.
Boots splash the water as people walk by,
The traffic is horrible and all give a sigh.

The rain continues into the night,
But everything is going to be all right.
Thunder and lightning can scare even you,
It also scares children and animals too.

The storm is upon us as we can see,
They say we need water and that may be.
Why does it come down so hard and steady?
But next time this happens, we will be ready.

Water makes flowers grow and hills turn green,
The most beautiful sight you've ever seen.
So be glad that the rain is here today,
As tomorrow will make it a better day.

Vacation Time

My boss gave me some vacation time,
But of course, I haven't even a dime.
Shall I go to the mountains or the sea?
Maybe I can get someone to go with me.

I know just where I will go,
I will stay at home, no one will know.
I can watch TV or read a book,
Play with my dog and even cook.

You don't need money to do these things,
Think of the happiness to me it brings.
I will feel rested after all is said and done,
As I rated this vacation as my number one.

I returned to work singing a song,
They asked me if anything was wrong.
I smiled and said that everything was fine,
I am doing it again on my next vacation time.

My Valentine

I had a little time and I wanted to spend some money,
It's Valentine's Day and I wanted something for you, honey.
I went to some clothing stores and some sport stores too,
I just couldn't find anything that was good enough for you.

So I stopped at some other stores and to my dismay,
There was nothing I could find for you for this special day.
I was very tired of walking, as shopping wears me out,
If I didn't buy anything, you'd just sit and pout.

Then I remembered just how much in love we really are,
I knew what I should give to you, for you are my shining star.
I got my list together and went on a spree,
This would be the best gift that you would ever see.

I came home to decorate and make sure everything was fine,
For I wanted you to know that you're my favorite valentine.
I gave you your gift and you were pleased as can be,
You cleaned your plate of the meal especially cooked by me.

My Little Snowman

There is a cute little snowman in my yard, so I'm told,
I looked out my window and this little guy looked so cold.
I am only six, but I knew that I loved him right away,
I waited for my parents to wake so I can go and play.

I saw that he had no scarf or hat, not even shoes or coat,
I knew my parents built him, but I think they missed the boat.
Bounded out of my room, grabbed some clothes and then,
I dressed warm as I wanted clothes on my little friend.

Got Dad's favorite hat and it covered that top bald patch,
He even had some shoes and everything was a match.
I took my mother's coat, but this man was hard to shape,
So I exchanged my mother's coat for her favorite cape.

When my folks finally go up, I could hear my mother scream,
I thought that maybe she was having a very terrible dream.
Then I heard my dad yell my name and I wondered why,
They ran out, stopped and smiled, they loved this little guy.

Wondrous Cycle

I saw a little hummingbird outside my window today,
He was flapping his tiny wings so fast then he flew away.
Soon he was back again drinking sap with his pointed beak,
I was so enthralled in watching that I could barely speak.

He was such a little thing, how can he survive?
I guess he has to move so fast just stay alive.
I thought about small children playing in the sun,
And then I wondered how this world really had begun.

It really doesn't matter the theory that you use,
But the animal kingdom knows they all shall pay their dues.
Flowers around us seem to die and some bloom again,
Each has its own cycle of life, including the life of Man.

Weather

I've never seen the rain fall with such force,
But I have seen the flowers drink and grass turn green.
I have not seen the snow fall so long, but of course,
I live in a place where mostly the sun is seen.

I've never seen everything so clean as it is today,
But now I can see that falling rain made it so.
I have never seen the traffic so light on the freeway,
This kind of day, I want to get in my car and go.

I have never heard the wind whistle so strong,
It shakes the whole house as it passes by.
It's really scary, but don't get me wrong,
I respect the wind, so I just give a long sigh.

I have never seen the sun so bright,
I love to lie in it for just a little while.
Some say it may impair my sight,
I wear sunglasses, put lotion on my skin, and smile.

The Ocean of Love

To the ocean lovers

Young children run on the beach toward the ocean blue
When the water touches them they don't know what to do.
They play tag with the ocean laughing and crying all the way
Then they're right back at it and they keep it up all day.
Waves change constantly to an almost a level plane
So smooth and so peaceful then a big one comes again.
When it comes crashing down with its foam so white
It's magnificent but almost scary as another is in sight.
Strong and powerful tides brings this beauty to our land
Tides are strange and wonderful but hard to understand.
They can be strong and treacherous dangerous as can be
If one isn't careful they could be carried out to sea.
Some use the ocean for pleasure or to make a livelihood
The fishermen sell the fish they catch which is understood.
Sometime the water is very calm sea breezes blow above
When this land was put here it must have been with love.

When the Sky Is Crying

To those who are depressed with the weather

After a long hot summer trees and plants begin to die
Animals are thirsty when the sky begins to cry.
Tears are rain and snow that come from high above
When the sky cries its tears they are mixed with love.
When the sky is crying we try to come inside
And when a strong wind blows then we try to hide.
If the sky cries constantly we don't know what to do
We get all excited and we start complaining too.
When the sky is cold its tears are very white
And as the snow falls on the land its such a lovely sight.
Some trees and plants come alive and they begin to grow
They are strong and healthy from all the rain and snow.
So if black clouds are forming high up in the sky
That's an indication that the sky is about to cry.
When the sky is crying don't feel sad by the tears
Because it makes life and love last for years and years.

Our Great Seasons

Spring is such a wondrous thing
The flowers bloom and tiny birds sing
There are sprinkles of rain and rainbows too
New life is awakened and all seems so new.

Summer is warmer during most of these days
We feel the warmth of it in many ways
It brings us energy we just can't explain
We travel by car or ship or fly in a plane.

Fall is the thoughtful time of the year
The leaves change colors and fall like a tear
It's beautiful and calm and relaxes the mind
Cool days and nights are restful and kind.

Winter is known as the coldest of all
The strong wind blows and snowflakes fall
It brings excitement for young and for old
Holidays are special even when it's so cold.

Nature's Birthday

You truly are a nature's joy,
You are the sea and sky,
You treat your plants like a precious toy,
And the flowers you plant never die.

The wind that blows, the rain that falls
Spread colors throughout our land,
The sun and snow on a treetop calls,
For a warm and welcome hand.

We extend our hand, our dear ole friend,
Please stay the way you are,
May all your birthdays keep that trend
Of being our guiding star.

Every day is your special day.

Have You Ever Seen?

To those who take things for granted

Have you ever seen such a pretty sunrise
The blend of colors in the heavens' skies?
The world waking up from a restful night
Have you ever looked at this wonderful sight?

Have you ever seen such a beautiful day?
Everything stirring in a busy way
Working, playing, and driving around
Have you ever heard that marvelous sound?

Have you ever seen setting sun from the blue?
This beautiful time is made for you
Colors streak the sky, takes your breath away
Have you ever watched the end of the day?

Have you ever seen such a wondrous night?
The stars are out and the moon is bright
Hear the soft wind as it forces you to rest
Have you ever realized that this is the best?

The Desert Rats

My friends, the desert rats

Sunrise in the desert is beautiful, calm, and fair
When colors splash across the sky, nothing can compare.
The sunsets are as lovely with colors that are bright
When wildflowers are blooming, everything is just right.
All the people are friendly and considerate as can be
They're known as desert rats and you can plainly see.
They love this land of hot and cold and they are happy too
They won't live anywhere else as each day is something new.
Many sports are played in this lovely desert land
Tennis and golf are popular, which is easy to understand.
The golf courses are abundant and turfs are very green
The country clubs are full when the golfers play eighteen.
During the long, hot summer, people try to stay inside
They don't want to leave and some haven't even tried.
So when you visit the desert, be careful or you will find
The desert gets under your skin and always on your mind.

Your Special Gift

There is a special tree that stands tall and straight,
Its branches are heavy with limbs, but it doesn't break.
Many people sit beneath that tree because they love it so,
And once you are sitting there, you never want to go.

Some read, some are alone, sometimes you see two lovers,
That tree bring happiness to them and to all the others.
I saw some animals playing beneath that lovely tree,
You could tell that they were happy and contented as can be.

No one knows who planted it or how long it's even been there,
But no one will destroy it as the people really care.
If you haven't seen a special tree, you can find one if you try,
Did you pay attention or did you just pass right on by?

When you are walking in the countryside or just down the street,
Please take a look around you and the beauty that you seek.
You'll see green grass and flowers and a special tree or two,
That is your special gift that was freely given to you.

PART THREE

TECHNOLOGY

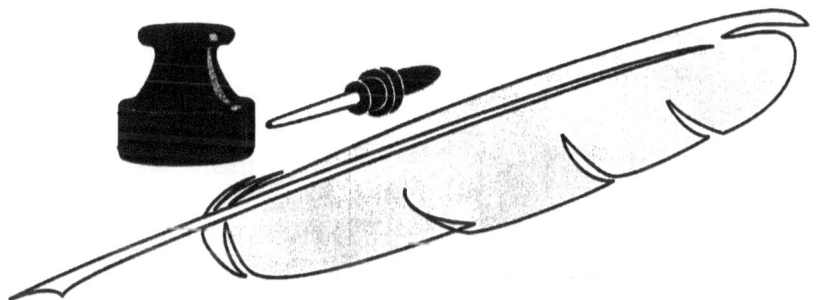

My Little Computer

As I sit at my computer wondering what to write,
I look around my little room that is cheery and so bright.
I began to wonder what others are doing on this fine day,
My mind begins to wander and my fingers begins to play.

I stop what I am doing and play a game or two,
I don't get much work done and believe me, that is true.
I get started on a little game and I won't stop until I win,
This little computer wears me out, and now I'm all in.

I stop for lunch, of course, I haven't written a line,
My stomach now is growling, so that big lunch is mine.
After I have eaten, I get sleepy and tired too,
My mind becomes a blank; does this ever happen to you?

I might as well log off as I won't get much done,
Telephone rings and the caller wants us to have some fun.
I would like to do that 'cause she's a good friend of mine,
But I looked at my lonely computer and knew I had to decline.

My Remote

I turned on my new TV today to see what I could find,
I punched my remote as news was on my mind.
Cartoons appeared, and children think they are great,
Another station showed an old movie made in '48.

I kept using my remote and this time it was a soap,
I didn't know what it was about and felt like a silly dope.
I flipped and then just guess what I have found,
The movie was so old, it didn't have any sound.

I clicked my remote again and someone was cooking food,
I tried to watch, but got hungry as it put me in the mood.
After my little snack, I flipped the remote once more,
But by now I forgot what I was really searching for.

With so many selections, how can anyone make a pick?
I'm glad there's a remote that makes everything so slick.
Whoever made this little thing made it so easy to use,
By the way, after flipping, I finally found the news.

Pat Davis

Television Sets

Have you ever looked at all the models and makes,
And all the different sizes and gadgets it takes?
This one has this and another has that,
How do you know just where you are at?

If you like a big screen, it costs you much more,
If your house is small, you'll sit on the floor.
But just think of the entertainment you'll get
With a brand-new fancy television set!

In my life I've purchased quite a few,
But now I really don't know what's new.
I love that TV, there is no doubt,
I am sometimes lost when the cable goes out.

It can entertain and inform you of news of the day,
If I didn't have one, I would buy one today.
So if my TV ever goes on the blink,
I would buy another as quick as a wink!

Hear Ye, Hear Ye!

Hear ye, hear ye! I am having a big sale,
Only a penny a piece for this wonderful junk mail.
Corporations, companies, and little businesses too,
You may have your pick, it's only a penny to you.

You can haul it away for a penny a pick,
You can trust me, as this is no trick.
Some are from companies I never knew,
This piece of junk mail must be for you.

Hear ye, hear ye! I will prevail
To sell this precious new junk mail.
I am going on vacation so I can get a grip,
I must get away and go on a trip.

Every day the mail seems to grow,
Different companies are now asking for dough.
I'm selling it cheap in this wonderful sale,
Please, won't you buy my precious junk mail?

Our New Car

We just purchased a brand-new car,
Drove it on the road, but not too far.
All the new gadgets and buttons to press,
What they are used for is anyone's guess.

Whatever happened to a simple machine?
You just turned the key and left the scene.
No buttons to push or directions to read,
No lights to watch or warning sounds to heed.

They all say that improvements were made,
It should have been better for the price we paid.
A switch to move the mirrors both up and down,
Another one to move the seats to the ground.

Before we fill up this special gas tank,
We will have to stop by at our local bank.
Don't get me wrong, we love this car,
But you must be a college graduate to drive it far.

Telephone Calls

The telephone calls are driving me wild,
The company starts out meek and mild.
Then after a strong sales pitch or two,
They think they've really gotten to you.

But once you say no, that should be enough,
But that is when they start to get rough.
They pretend they never heard of that word no,
Still they persist and won't let you go.

You try to be nice, but to no avail,
They keep on trying to make a sale.
Some say that it won't cost you a dime,
That's true; it costs more, including your time.

They keep at you until you demand,
What part of no don't you understand?
I am a very happy person most of the time,
Maybe I'll contribute some other time.

Automation

To those who can relate

Have you ever tried to place a call?
You hear a recording and they have the gall
To tell you to press one, two, three or four,
It comes on again and you press more.

The music then begins to play
And then the recording starts to say
How important that you really are,
But then you're asked to press the star.

Another recording comes along
And says that you have done it wrong.
So you hang up and try again
You press the numbers and count to ten.

You've yet to hear a human voice
There's no service and we have no choice.
If you have a question and you have to call,
Forget it, 'cause you'll reach no one at all.

That Little Cell

To those with the little cell

Nothing is more important as a cell phone by our ear
You can buy them anywhere, so there's no need to fear.
Buy them at all department stores or at any mall
We can't live without them, as we must make that call.
Young and old are talking, you see them everywhere
Shopping, driving, or eating, they don't seem to care.
We use it to keep our businesses alive and well
Important problems can be solved over this little cell.
We can monitor our children from wherever we may be
And the cell phone is needed in case of an emergency.
Be aware to what's around you if you drive or you will fall
If you have a fatal accident, this cell won't help you at all.

This Little Card

Time to celebrate, time to cheer,
Because your birthday is very near.
You may have a cake and a party too.
This little card wishes the best for you.

Time to dance, time to play,
There's not much else anyone can say.
Money is scarce, can't buy you a gift,
Hope this little card will give you a lift.

Time for laughter, time to sing,
A birthday song to you friends bring.
You may have waited all year through,
This little card shows thoughts of you.

Time to wave, time to go,
With a smile of love, you should know
You're thought about the whole year through
This little card shows love for you.

PART FOUR

BELIEFS

Your Belief

Some people look at the dark side of life and they live it,
Some are negative all through their life and they live it.
Others believe they will be sick and they are,
Still, others believe they will be unhappy and they are.

Some people look at the bright side of life and they live it,
Some are positive all through their life and they live it.
Others believe they will be strong and well and they are,
Still, others believe they will be happy and they are.

So remember, my friends, what you believe is what
you will be, and what you will be is what you believe.

Some People Say

They say that money doesn't buy happiness.
Smiling, I reply that they don't know where to shop.
They say that money is the root of all evil,
That means that overspending must stop.

They say we have too much time on our hands,
So let's find them a job right away.
They say that people drive much too fast,
We need to stop those drivers today.

They say our government is falling apart,
Then we must move in a new direction.
They say that democracy is no longer strong,
We can fix it at the time of election.

They say that we're running out of time,
We know that it's not hopeless, do not despair.
They say that our country is in trouble,
But we know there's nothing we can't repair.

Being Wise Brings Happiness

You don't need to spend money to have a friend or two.
You don't need to have sadness before they come to you.
So take this advice and a much happier life you'll live,
And you'll get back much more than you'll ever give.

There is an old saying everyone can understand.
It is known and practiced throughout our glorious land.
If you do not believe in it, you will surely be defeated.
It simply says, "Treat others as you wish to be treated."

Greatest Sound of All

What is the greatest sound you've ever heard?
Is it a babbling brook or a tweeting little bird?
Maybe it's someone singing a favorite tune,
Or is it the wedding bells ringing in June?

What is the greatest sound you've ever heard?
Is it the sound of thunder? But that's absurd.
Perhaps it's the horn from faraway ships,
Or after you cooked a meal, someone smacking their lips.

What is the greatest sound you've ever heard?
Is it the roar of hoofs from a large cattle herd,
Or is it the sound of a party, all having fun?
It might be someone saying that you are the one.

What is that greatest sound you hear?
That question I can answer without a fear,
It's the laughter of children throughout our land,
That is God's greatest gift that was given to Man.

Thankful

I saw a man sitting on a bench with his goods in a cart,
I walked toward him; what I saw put a pain through my heart.
He was ragged and unshaven and his eyes showed such fright,
I wasn't sure if I should talk to him, as he was such a sight.

I knew he was homeless and he had nowhere to go,
I slowed down as I got closer and I wanted to help him so.
Our eyes met and I just then, I didn't know what to do,
I felt that any of us could be that man, even me and you.

I said "Hello" and he grinned and gave a smile,
I got out some money and gave it to him in a little pile.
He simply said, "Thank you" as he slowly stood up,
He was already counting the money as he put it in a cup.

Two children came up and hugged this little shaggy man,
They called him daddy and they just turned and ran.
He said how lucky he was and now he could buy some food,
He has so little, but still he put me in a thankful mood.

God's Wrath

The storm came up so quickly, it took us by surprise,
The wind blue so hard in the cloudy, darkened skies.
The cold rain came down so hard, we heard the water splash,
Then we heard the thunder and it came down with a crash.

"Do you think God is mad at us?" a girl was heard to say,
Her father said, "God gets angry in His own special way."
We wondered if it was anger He displayed that stormy night,
The more we thought about it, we knew the little girl was right.

Something had to awaken us before we do more wrong,
We want to keep our Earth alive, moral, and very strong.
Many mistakes were made through our land today,
Let us try to fix them fast before we go astray.

We forget about the beautiful birds up high in the sky,
And the animals and flowers which are beauty to the eye.
What we will remember is that horrible scary night,
When God had enough and He had to shed some light.

Health, Wealth, and Happiness

Health and happiness are the ingredients that I need,
May I make the money in payments or buy another deed?
I don't know where to buy them or the amount that I must pay,
If money can't buy those things, there is nothing more to say.

I can't live without them, maybe I am through,
If money can't buy happiness, I don't know what to do.
I am willing to spend my money on health to remain alive,
What ingredients shall I buy in order to survive?

I haven't been kind to my fellowman, that is very true,
I was busy making money, lost my health and happiness too.
The money is still there, but I am surely out of luck,
Because what I wanted more was that almighty buck.

I began to change my ways and helped others just in time,
I gained back my health and happiness by not spending a dime.
This is a big lesson that most of us need to know,
All can live in happiness if you don't just think of dough.

The Whisper

Sorry you lost someone you love
We know you'll miss them so
They just went to Heaven above
You can talk to them, you know.

A little whisper you may hear
When you are lonely or sad
"I'm in Heaven and it's lovely here."
You'll smile and say you're glad.

So just remember when you're blue
The whisper that came from above
Give thumbs up and a wink or two
And your special smile of love.

My Star

There is a tiny speck way up high,
It twinkles brightly in a darkened sky.
So steadfast and so beautiful too,
My star has a shine, just like it's new.
I look straight up and then I see
My shining star that's waiting for me.

I may sound crazy, and it may be so,
I see it smiling, then it starts to go
As a blanket of clouds passes by, and then,
A moment later, it's back again.
I say good night and give it a smile,
For I'll see it again in a little while.

Years go by and it's still shining bright,
Waiting for me to say good night.
Now I am old and need glasses to see,
My star and I, together we'll be.
So when I am gone to Heaven above,
I'll be with my star that I so love.

Positive Attitude

I sit in my chair and look at the ocean and city lights below,
That peace is always with me, no matter where I go.
I glance up at the billowy clouds as the sun sinks in the sea,
Sky streaked with bright colors is spectacular to me.
I wish to share the happiness I possess every day,
You can find that contentment in your own special way.
Animals awaken and birds stretch their wings in sky above,
As a new day begins and ends with everlasting love.
I have a little saying that I repeat to all I might see,
To find that peace of mind is really simple as can be.
Some people think negative thoughts as we know they do,
But if you look for something positive, you will find that too.
So my friends, when you become very sad or blue,
Look at life in a positive way and happiness will come to you.
You may have a very tough life, no matter what you try,
But keep a positive attitude and you'll smile instead of cry.

PART FIVE

TRAVEL

Pat Davis

Troops in War

The troops were slowly walking to the noisy front lines,
Carrying heavy gear and fear and was on their minds.
Some don't know why they're in this desolate land,
Others seem to know and they really understand.

They see their comrades fall as they begin this walk,
The tears began to flow; it's quiet, there is no talk.
They think about their loved ones they had left behind,
Fingers tighten on the weapons to face this hateful grind.

Those at home are worrying and wondering where they are,
Our loved ones and friends are a special shining star.
The home front has not forgotten their loved ones, not at all,
When our troops come home, there will be happiness for all.

So please bring the troops home as quickly as you can,
Let's bring them to their families, each and every man.
We have fought in many wars to protect the USA,
When we defeat them, there'll be happiness that day.

Clickety-Clack, Clickety-Clack

The passengers were loading into the cars
The conductor was there wearing gold bars
All then were seated and tickets were taken
They checked them all so they weren't mistaken.

The luggage was placed in a big rack
Clickety-clack, clickety-clack

All the tickets were placed in a big stack
Clickety-clack, clickety-clack

People are leaving, some may come back
Clickety-clack, clickety-clack

The sound of the train roared down the track
Clickety-clack, clickety-clack

It brought everyone safely back
Clickety-clack, clickety-clack

If you ever go on a little train ride
I will be with you at your side
That's about the only way I will travel around
As I want to hear that special sound
Clickety-clack, clickety-clack.

My Daily Walk

I jumped from my bed this morning to go for my daily walk.
I met some people on the way and we stopped to talk.
We talked about the weather and the news of the day.
More joined us and we listened to what they had to say.

We have such nice neighbors that go out of their way
To stop and greet others by saying that it's a lovely day.
Some are walking their dogs, others are jogging along,
All are smiling and happy as if nothing was ever wrong.

I enjoy my walks in the morning just as the sun peaks out.
That's the best time for me, of that there is no doubt.
Walking is good for the soul and many say that's true,
And it's good for everyone, which includes me and you.

The air is fresh and clean and walking keeps you very fit.
You'll feel so much happier and you'll never want to quit.
I hope you follow this advice and keep on walking as I do,
I know you'll enjoy yourself and become much healthier too.

The Sheriff

A man was riding through a lonely, desolate land,
His gun in his holster, the bridle in his hand.
His spurs were off so it was a quiet ride,
He checked to see if his saddle bags were tied.

Killing this man was planted in his brain,
He had to stop him for inflicting so much pain.
He glanced at a star that was pinned upon his chest,
He was very confident, he knew he was the best.

The town was in sight, he began to step up the pace,
He became nervous; a solemn look was on his face.
The saloon was open, so he came through the door,
And when the sheriff left, a dead man was on the floor.

So if you see a rider searching for a man,
His gun in his holster and a bridle in his hand,
And a shining star that is placed upon his chest,
That is the sheriff and he still knows he's the best.

PART SIX

DITTY/STORIES

Pat Davis

Shopping Spree
(A Ditty)

It's a beautiful day to go shopping,
Many stores we shall be stopping.
They are having a big sale,
We'll shop without fail,
Which means money, we will be dropping.

Time

*Time is the most important measurement that we have today.
We can't do anything or go anywhere without it.
What did we do before watches were invented? Everything
and everybody is involved with time. Today, some even need
to get it down to seconds and milliseconds.*

*There are sayings about it, such as, "Don't put off
tomorrow what you can do today." "Time marches on." There are
so many seconds left to play. "Time heals all wounds," etc.
Appointments, work, school, and much more need a
start time and some need end times, too.*

*Would there be anything positive in our lives if we didn't
have a clock to watch? Perhaps the answer the that
question is that it would put chaos in our land. Of course,
one positive instance that I can think of is that no one would ever
be late for anything. Still another positive might be that we
wouldn't know any time of day it would be or how much
longer would we wait for darkness.*

*Think of how often it would effect your life, and maybe then
we can be grateful that time is on our side.*

Pat Davis

The Concerned Bystander

*A man came upon an accident and stopped to help. He looked
inside and there was a small child in a car seat who looked up
at him and smiled. He was so shocked he just grinned
and lifted the little one to safety, talking to the child.
The child was laughing now, so the man knew he was okay.
He set the car seat by the road and returned to the
other car. He tried to get a response, but heard nothing.*

*He called 911 and reported what he had found as he tried to
check a pulse, but he couldn't reach them in the car.
He waited such a long time for more help to come, when he heard
the siren, he felt easier. The little baby made no sound.*

*The paramedics got the people out of the car and to the helper's
surprise, he saw his mother and father being carried out. He was
expecting them to attend a family dinner that night. It seems
that a car cut them off and his father slammed on the brakes which
made the car flip.*

*The paramedics found that they were both okay as they began to
talk and when they saw their son, they asked if they were late for
dinner. Their son laughed and said that they would have to warm it.*

*The family got checked out at the hospital and everyone was happy,
and as they shared the warmed over dinner, the mother said
that even after a tragedy, there can be a happy ending.*

Realization!

A couple went to the casino to have some fun but they
took the money that they were saving to buy a car. They
knew taking the money was not a good idea because the car
was old and not very safe. Having fun was much more
important to this couple than anything else regardless of
the consequences. They gambled away all their savings and
continued to write checks to get more cash so they could
have more fun. The next day they were mentally exhausted.

Misguided?

When they got home they had to borrow a car as the
old one was not running. They were so tired from
gambling that neither wanted to go to work.
They thought if they borrowed more money they'd be
happy once again. The couple became so miserable that
they couldn't get along with one another but they
still believed money bought happiness and since they
had none they felt that lack of money was the reason.

Misguided?

They begin to think how happy they were when they first got
married. But they had no money just love for one another.
They finally realized how happy they were to not only find
one another but how they lived their daily lives.

Realization and Success!

The Wise Woodsman

Many years ago, a woodsman started to cut down the most beautiful tree in the forest. He had sharpened his axe and was ready to cut it down so he could build a big house for his family where this tree was standing straight and tall.

He started to swing his axe but stopped as he heard the birds high above him. He heard his young son say, "Dad, there are birds in this tree. You can't cut it down now!" He knew his son would remember how he had and killed innocent birds. "You're right, son, this has to wait." His son adored him and smiled, and at that moment, his son thought he was the greatest father ever.

Time passed and it was early summer and the father went back to the same tree to cut it down for his new house. Once again, he started to swing, but stopped and remembered how his son looked at him with such adoring eyes, and at that moment, he knew he could never destroy such a beautiful thing. He saw a clearing with logs on the ground and immediately, he started to build his house.

He went home that night and told his family that he had started to build their house by the tree for protection from the elements. He told his son that he must always remember that a person doesn't have to destroy in order to build. There was much happiness in the farmhouse from then on.

PART SEVEN

SPORTS

Pat Davis

The Newcomer

The golf course was ready and players were by the cup,
They were swinging their clubs now for a longer warmup.
As they called the first golfer to go to the tee,
He was very excited, as the golf course he could see.

They called his name and he teed his ball,
He swung hard and the ball flew long and tall.
The next golfer that was in line teed his ball as well,
He swung at it and hit it and knew that it was swell.

And so it went as each player tried to get a low score,
The golfers were tied and had to play some more.
All who played that day saw that golf ball roll,
They were smiling when they came to the playoff hole.

The pros thought the ball would come close to the hole,
It just didn't happen, as the course was taking its toll.
Then a newcomer came up to see what he could do,
A hole in one! Then he knew the others were through.

It's Only a Game

Football was played on a field that was frozen.
The coin was tossed and the goals were chosen.
The ball was kicked and they began to play.
The crowd went wild on that very cold day.

Men were being tackled by the opposing team.
A man was hurt and the crown did scream.
The quarterback tossed the ball in the air,
But the other team got it, it was ruled fair.

So it continued, either team could have won,
Back and forth it went, but all were having fun.
It is a territorial thing, some would say,
And I only thought that it's a game they play.

So if you are ever watching a football game,
You'll see some men that may come up lame.
You'll find out they'd rather play in the sun,
But thankful they carry a ball instead of a gun.

The Wise Hunter

To all wise hunters

The mountains were shaded dark blue and green
Their beautiful snow tops added to the scene.
Icy streams trickled down steep mountainside
Animals were looking for a better place to hide.
The hunter came upon them with a rifle in his hand
He was hunting some animals that lived in this land.
He raised his rifle high when he heard the bushes tear
He started to pull the trigger when he saw a baby bear.
He lowered his rifle and just stopped and stared
Thought of his own son and how much he really cared.
He could never shoot a cub as he was a father too
Then a large bear arrived to see what he could do.
The hunter was very quiet and did not move at all
The bears began to play and they were having a ball.
He then realized just what it was he was seeing
Love exists in all life not just in a human being.

PART EIGHT

PUZZLES

Jigsaw Puzzle of Life

There's a strange jigsaw puzzle waiting to be solved,
Pieces are scattered, but you become involved.
You pick up a piece and try to fit it in just right,
But this jigsaw puzzle of life is putting up a tough fight.
So you try another piece, hoping this one will fit,
You turn it this way and that, thinking that this is it.
Just as life has twists and turns that you follow along,
This puzzle can't be put together if these pieces are all wrong.
You've got the frame together and you're as happy as can be,
But inside the shell, it's slow going as you will readily see.
You'll get annoyed, but you'll find a piece every now and then,
As you try to force a piece in place, it pops right out again.
Years go by and you'll wonder if it will be whole once more,
This puzzle is different than any others you've done before.
When you are old and tired and ready to leave this land,
Put in the last piece and complete this puzzle as planned.

Which One Are You?

There is a narrow path that all shall follow to reach life's destination. There are many turns and twists as well as a few dead ends. As you walk down this path of life, you will learn your fate; whether it's good or bad depends on you.

Some think that they will suffer and find dismay, and they will. Some think of it as a glorious thing and might even walk a little faster to reach their goal of happiness and peace, and they will find it.

Which one are you?

Still, others hesitate to go down this path of life and are confused when they see the small paths shooting off in different directions. They will always wonder if they had taken the right path. But others cannot wait to see what is around the next bend to find more love and joy.

Which one are you?

This path continues throughout our lives, no matter who or where we are. Eventually there will be an end to this path, but how we walk it will decide if we will be content or miserable.

Which one are you?

Love Is?

For all those who try to define it

Love is a feeling of brotherhood toward others
And the feelings of siblings, fathers, or mothers.
All animals and plants have this capacity too
But no one can understand why we do the things we do.
Love is an emotion that is very strong at best
It makes us warm and tender, it's better than the rest.
This affection is caring about people we don't know
It's a feeling about objects and some define it so.
Love is a worldwide phenomenon that's hard to explain
Does it come from the heart or maybe from the brain?
Where does it come from and where or why does it go?
There's no way to answer, but we all need it so.
Love is a magic that all want to take and give
It's something marvelous; without it, we wouldn't live.
It is strange and wonderful and that is very true
But how we say and handle it is up to me and you.

Another New Adventure

If something happens and we're not prepared
Let's not get excited, upset, or scared,
For this is definitely our lucky day,
As another new adventure has come our way.

New things happen all our life long,
That's what makes us courageous and strong.
How boring life would be if it's the same every day,
And if another new adventure didn't come our way.

We all have problems, that's a known fact,
So let us get together and make a strong pact.
When problems come up, we all need to say
That another new adventure has come our way.

We can handle any problems that may come about,
No need to yell, cry, or even shout.
We'll roll up our sleeves and face come what may,
And enjoy the new adventure that has come our way.

PART NINE

LIGHTHOUSES

The Lighthouse of Life

To all lighthouse keepers

There is a beautiful lighthouse that is high upon a bluff
Seamen head for the light whenever the sea gets rough.
One day the fog was thick and the surf was very strong
Hard to keep the ship on course, made the day seem long.
The frightened crew was nervous as they approached the bay
What was going to happen at the close of this fateful day?
Storm was getting stronger, the waves were splashing high
The ship was sinking fast when they saw a lighted sky.
They fought harder now to get closer to the shore
This crew was so exhausted, all were tired to the core.
It was very dark, but they saw that beam of light
All on board were grateful for that patch of sky so bright.
They set sail toward the beam, but they were almost drowned
They all loved that lighthouse and the safety they had found.
So when you see a lighthouse, think of all those it did save
If it hadn't been for this light, they'd be in a watery grave.

My Love for Lighthouses

There is an old abandoned lighthouse that stands upon a hill,
It was once a tourist attraction but now it's quiet and still.
The walls have crumbled down and left only a shell,
My heart was nearly broken when that structure fell.
I stood before the lighthouse and looked out toward the sea,
I turned and glanced upward for the light that used to be.
My heart was very sad and my eyes welled up with tears,
For it had saved many seamen throughout its many years.
Beacons danced on the sea and kissed many decks and sails,
Some lighthouses have rotted away and now darkness prevails.
One can hear the waves crashing on the rocks below,
But there's no special light to tell travelers where to go.
Some lighthouses are still standing very tall and bright,
Doing what they do best by lighting up the night.
Some are bed and breakfast which is hard to understand,
For the light tells men on ships how close they are to land.
When you visit a working lighthouse be grateful as can be,
For you have seen something special as it's part of history.
So my friends be aware that whatever you might do,
Please enjoy all of them that are waiting just for you.

PART TEN

MISCELLANEOUS

The Policeman

A policeman came to see me today.
I answered the door and I heard him say,
"We have a report that you've been bad."
I looked at him and I was mad.

I have been good both day and night,
I slammed the door and locked it tight.
He rang the bell and yelled through the door
To open it up and he'll tell me more.

It was my birthday and I'm seven today,
I told him my dad would be here right away.
He was getting a good job and he was a good man,
I will wait for him as long as I can.

The voice said, "I'm kidding in fun,
I am your dad and you are my son."
I opened the door and clearly did I choke,
It was my dad playing a happy birthday joke.

Good Ole USA

I paid my income and property tax too,
I am depressed, but there's nothing I can do.
I wanted to revolt and I didn't want to pay,
But I am thankful because I live in the USA.

I smiled and took a long look around,
I was so glad I lived on this great ground.
So I don't feel bad when I have to pay,
'Cause we are free and live in the USA.

And when I feel I just can't get ahead,
I don't give up and take to my bed.
I am so grateful, I'm happy to say,
That I live in the good ole USA today.

Other countries are poor as they can be,
I do not want this to happen to me.
I love this country with all my heart,
And from this land I will never depart.

Hair

Have you ever had a bad hair day,
You spray it and it still won't stay?
You set your hair and it doesn't take,
So you get it cut and what a mistake.

You wash it and brush it until you're sore,
It doesn't work, so you brush some more.
You massage you head and it feels good, no doubt,
When you change the shampoo, the color comes out.

Why do some people have beautiful hair?
Still others need some special care.
That is a puzzle that cannot be solved,
Unless you get a beautician involved.

But do not be sad and don't be blue,
Your hair will become beautiful too.
If you just keep healthy, wealthy, and wise,
You'll have beautiful hair as advertised.

The Captain and His Dog Toot

To those who love the ocean

There was a retired sea captain sitting on the sand
He watched some ships sailing by that were tall and grand.
He remembered how anxious he was just to go to sea
When he got his commission, he was proud as he could be.
He was always with his little dog, Toot, a loyal friend indeed
If in danger, he would bark and this captain learned to heed.
Toot loved it on the bridge, thought he was in command
He wagged his tail and got excited when a sailor spotted land.
Years have passed since this captain sailed the ocean blue
But he would go to sea in a second, as that is what he knew.
Most would see an old man with a little dog in the sun
Still, others talked to him and learned what they had done.
They sat on the beach for many years as the seasons change
But now that place is empty and it seems so very strange.
As the ships pass that spot, they give a final salute
For they all loved this captain and his faithful little dog Toot.

Appreciate What We Have

There is a little package under the tree
I am only seven, but I think it's for me
It can't be from my mom or my dad
Golly, I want to open it bad.

It's wrapped up pretty, has a bow on it too
If it is not from Santa, then I wonder who?
My mom and my dad are in Heaven above
But the tag is signed with loads of love.

There's decorations all over this place
Why, there's even a little Santa Claus face
This orphan house has candy and treats
I am so glad I am not still on the streets.

It's time to run to the beautiful tree
I am going to open this package to me
It's a little blue blanket so I won't be cold
I will keep it forever, even when I am old.

Your Mystery Book

Just to live is an exciting thing
You never know what life will bring.
It's like a large mystery book
Turn the pages and take a look.
You'll see many chapters I am sure
Some chapters in life will be hard to endure.
But others you will find are wonderful and true
And still other chapters shows happiness too.
Words are like the days that go flying by
You can't stop them no matter how you try.
There are more words than grains of sand
And as you read on you will understand.
Keep turning and read what comes next
This book is a mystery unlike a text.
Each book is different and you'll be involved
But the mystery of your life will never be solved.

PART ELEVEN

EPILOGUE

Epilogue

I hope you enjoyed these poems from my heart.
I hope you will heed these words from the start.
May you always find much more than less,
Then you'll find your own freeway to happiness.

www.ingramcontent.com/pod-product-compliance
Lightning Source LLC
Chambersburg PA
CBHW031237280526
45784CB00004B/1615